Wilson Reading System®

Stories for Older Students
Book Three
Steps 7-9

THIRD EDITION

by Jay Brown

Wilson Language Training Corporation

www.wilsonlanguage.com

**Wilson Reading System® Stories for Older Students
Book Three | Steps 7-9**

by Jay Brown

Item # STS789

ISBN 978-1-56778-129-8

THIRD EDITION (revised 2004)

PUBLISHED BY:

Wilson Language Training Corporation
47 Old Webster Road
Oxford, MA 01540
United States of America

(800) 899-8454

www.wilsonlanguage.com

Printed in the U.S.A.

October 2013

HESS100

Contents

Introduction

These stories are designed to accompany tutor and student through the six syllables that make up our English language. I have presented here a controlled progression of stories, each focusing on particular phonetic principles. As each new syllable type is presented, the previously studied syllables are brought forward to provide a constant review.

I have tried to combine disciplined writing with a little human interest, perhaps with a light humorous touch, and have provided each story with a theme that might be of interest to the older student.

I first wrote these pieces under the heading "Fun with Words." I have had fun, not without some agonizing, pushing the words around - groping for some, discarding many. I have found the readings helpful in my tutoring. I hope you and your students will have as much fun without the agony of composition, and will find the systematic progression helpful.

Format

In writing this collection of stories I have kept two goals in mind: to provide themes of interest to the older student and to stay within the range of the syllable types being studied at a specific level. The order of the presentation follows the Wilson Reading System sequence; the precepts are those of Orton-Gillingham. If whimsy or mystery creeps in, it is because the available words lead me there. Because long sentences tend to exhaust the learning reader, I have tried to keep them short, even jerky. For the same reason I have kept the length of the stories to one page or, in some cases, to one paragraph. Each story is composed of words reflecting a particular level. They progress through the six syllable types in the following sequence:

- **Closed**: A single vowel is followed (or closed off) by a consonant. Its vowel takes the short sound. (**hat, pet, in, romp, trust**)

- **Vowel-Consonant-e**: The terminal silent "e" renders the preceding single vowel long. (**came, bite, vote, eve, crude**)

- **Open**: There is no consonant following (or closing off) the single vowel. The vowel takes the long sound. (**he, go, repent**)

- **Consonant-le**: This three-letter, terminal syllable has a consonant followed immediately by **le**. The consonant and **l** are sounded. The **e** is silent. (**table, ripple, tackle**)

- **R-controlled**: The **r** determines the sound of its preceding vowel. (**bar, her, shirt, sort, hurt**)

- **Diphthongs/vowel digraphs**: Vowel combinations that make specific sounds. (**boy, see, way, how, out, wait, sea, bread**)

Sometimes, the English language defies the absolute rigidity of phonetic analysis. However, approximately 85% of English words can be decoded by phonetic and syllabic analysis. The remaining words must be acquired by sight, or by whole word memory. The irregular or "sight" words are printed at the top of each page unless they have been taught. The instructor may be called upon to help here because these are words the student is not expected to know. Also included are words with syllable types introduced in later steps. I have tried to keep to the level of the syllables being featured in each story, but occasionally a more advanced word slips in to provide some measure of sense, or just to keep the flow going. Such words also qualify for tutor assistance. The stories are listed by title in the table of contents and are grouped under the appropriate heading.

Editor's Note: The numbers in the lower corner of each page indicate the corresponding substep in the Wilson Reading System (WRS). For example, 1.6 relates to Step One, substep six in WRS. Use the WRS Scope and Sequence as a reference to determine if the story is appropriate for the student; the substeps included in this book are circled. All stories are intended for higher vocabulary students, so "B" appears after the Substep number in accordance with WRS.

Wilson Reading System Overview / Scope and Sequence of Word Structure

Step 1   Closed Syllables (3 Sounds)

1.1	**f, l, m, n, r, s,** (initial) and **d, g, p, t,** (final) **a, i, o** (Blending of 2 and 3 sounds)
1.2	**b, sh	u	h, j	c, k, ck	e	v, w, x, y, z	ch, th	qu, wh** (Introduced gradually)
1.3	Practice with above sounds (**wish, chop, wet**)
1.4	Double consonants, **all** (**bill, kiss, call**)
1.5	**am, an** (**ham, fan**)
1.6	Adding suffix -**s** to closed syllable words with 3 sounds (**bugs, chills**)

Step 2   Closed Syllables (4-6 Sounds)

2.1	**ang, ing, ong, ung, ank, ink, onk, unk** (**bang, pink**)
2.2	Closed syllables with blends: 4 sounds only + suffix -**s** (**bled, past, steps**)
2.3	Closed syllable exceptions: **ild, ind, old, ost, olt** (**mold, host**)
2.4	Five sounds in a closed syllable + suffix -**s** (**blend, trumps**)
2.5	Three-letter blends and up to 6 sounds in a closed syllable (**sprint, scrap**)

Step 3   Closed Syllables (Multisyllabic Words)

3.1	Two-syllable words with 2 closed syllables combined - no blends, schwa (**catnip, wagon**)
3.2	Two-syllable words with 2 closed syllables, including blends (**disrupt, fragment**)
3.3	Words with 2 closed syllables ending in **ct** blend (**contract, district**)
3.4	Multisyllabic words, combining only closed syllables (**Wisconsin, establish**)
3.5	-**ed**, -**ing** suffixes added to unchanging basewords with closed syllables (**slashing, blended**)

Step 4   Vowel-Consonant-e Syllable

4.1	Vowel-consonant-e syllable in one-syllable words (**hope, cave**)
4.2	Vowel-consonant-e syllable combined with closed syllables (**combine, reptile**)
4.3	Multisyllabic words combining 2 syllable types (**compensate, illustrate**)
4.4	**ive** exception: no word ends in **v** (**olive, pensive**)

Step 5   Open Syllable

5.1	Open syllable in one-syllable words, **y** as a vowel (**he, hi, shy**)
5.2	Open syllables combined with vowel-consonant-e and closed syllables in two-syllable words (**protect, decline**)
5.3	**y** as a vowel at the end of two-syllable words when combined with a closed syllable or another open syllable (**handy, pony**)
5.4	Multisyllabic words, combining 3 syllable types: open, closed, vowel-consonant-e (**instrument, amputate**)
5.5	**a** and **i** in unaccented, open syllables (**Alaska, indicate**)

Step 6   Suffix Endings (Unchanging Basewords) and Consonant-le Syllable

6.1	Suffix endings -**er**, -**est**, -**en**, -**es**, -**able**, -**ish**, -**y**, -**ive**, -**ly**, -**ty**, -**less**, -**ness**, -**ment**, -**ful** added to unchanging basewords (**thankful, classy**)
6.2	Suffix ending -**ed** (/**d**/, /**t**/) added to unchanging basewords (**thrilled, punished**)
6.3	Combining 2 suffixes to an unchanging baseword (**constructively, helpfulness**)
6.4	Stable final syllable: consonant-le, **stle** exception (**dribble, whistle**)

Cecil

Cecil recently moved from Boston to Cincinnati. He has Boston ancestry and a trace of a Boston accent. He has been a sincere Celtic fan since he was a kid.

Cecil lives in the basement of a hotel in the city. The hotel is adjacent to the public plaza and ice rink with excellent access to shopping. The space is small, almost twice as long as it is wide. It is not fancy living, but it is decent and at a price Cecil can handle. It is a nice place. Cecil calls it his cell, and his friends call him "Prince of the Cell." Mice have visited him once or twice, but he does not mind.

Cecil gets up at about 6:00 a.m. and gets himself a citrus drink, a slice of melon, and a cinnamon bun. He rides his bicycle to his job at City Hall. He is a census taker for the City of Cincinnati. He thinks life in the city is a rat race, but the job is a cinch. He is a fine citizen.

Cecil has had a little romance with a gal named Grace. They and his friends, Bruce and Lucy, go to the cinema or to dances from time to time. When Bruce, Lucy, and Grace visit Cecil at his place in the evening, they drink cider and tune in the Celtic games. With the Celtics on the tube and Grace by his side, life in Cincinnati is not bad.

age = /ij/

Gene and Ginny

Gene and Ginny live in a cottage at the edge of the village. Gene has a job at the Pine Ridge plant. It is a huge plant that makes luggage. His job is to manage the budget at the plant. Gene will send a message to the big boss to suggest changes that will cut costs. He has to salvage what he can of damaged luggage. The damage is mostly just a bent hinge. One of his jobs in the plant is to adjust the line voltage to prevent damage to the engines. A stoppage will upset the plant budget.

Ginny is a successful sales agent and makes excellent wages. Ginny sometimes has lunch with Gene at a small place where they can engage in a little chitchat. Lunch is apt to be a sandwich or a cabbage salad with a wedge of lemon and a chunk of fudge.

They drive an old truck that gets bad mileage, has slippage in the linkage and a clutch that does not always engage. Age has taken its toll, and the truck has a whole range of strange problems. At this stage it is not likely that the old wreck will pass the next registry test. Gene and Ginny must trade-up to a new truck.

Sludge

Sam Rutledge lived with his wife Madge and six kids in an old hunting lodge at the edge of a mill pond. Sam acted as judge of local disputes and also kept the village tax ledgers. Their kids swam in the pond from June to late fall and skated on it when it froze.

Dave Smith and his wife Bridget lived alone across the pond from the Rutledges. To help with his family's budget, Dave sold logs that he split with his sledgehammer and wedge. The Rutledges and the Smiths made a pledge of friendship to help in their lives on the mill pond.

In the spring, the bottom of the pond had to be dredged of sludge that ran down from the hills. Dave said the Rutledges used the pond almost exclusively, and he refused to share the cost of the dredging. He was a crusty old codger and refused to budge. Sam did not like to badger him on the matter. The grudge drove a wedge in their friendship. Bridget Smith visited Madge with plates of homemade fudge to try to bridge the gap. She would nudge Madge and tell her that Dave sometimes acted like a full-fledged curmudgeon but was truly a kind and gentle man. It was sad that the sludge was erasing the pledge of friendship.

Tracking the Phantom

To crack the drug ring, Ralph and Phil had to catch Dutch "The Phantom" Jackson. The men in graphics had provided photographs of the Phantom. Phil's job was to spot him by the photograph, plant hidden microphones, snatch him and fetch him back to Boston. The final phase of the chase led them to Nantucket.

There was one glitch in the plan: someone had switched photographs. The photo Phil had in his pocket was of a noted Nantucket magistrate. Phil had just been dispatched to Nantucket and was sure to pick up the magistrate.

Ralph had to stop Phil. He snatched up the kitchen phone and called Phil. He let the phone ring ten times as the clock ticked off the seconds. No answer. Ralph then phoned the Red Dolphin Grill at the dock where Phil was likely to be. Phil was not there. He then called the Pink Elephant Pub. Phil came on the line with wild music in the distance. He had lost track of time and missed the last ship home from Nantucket.

Ralph was quick to scratch the plan. He had been lucky to catch Phil in time to stop what would have been a drastic mistake. Still, he was angry to find Phil doing his hunting at the Pink Elephant Pub.

Becky Phelps

Becky Phelps ran home from class. All the kids in class were icky, she had lost her jacket and one sock, and she was sick of the alphabet. In Phys. Ed. she had won the hopscotch trophy, and in graphics class she got an A in sketching. But her grades on the alphabet tests were rotten. All those little black sticks and scribbles jumped about on the page like bugs. Ms. Fitch said the letters should tell her things, and that she would help Becky after class. Becky liked second grade for most things but not for the alphabet.

Tom Phelps is Becky's older brother and is in Mr. Phelon's fifth grade class. His best friend, Mitch, pitches for their ball games and is also the fastest in track. Tom helps Mitch at home with his English. Mitch is quick with math, but the letters give him a bad time.

Mitch and Becky get along fine. They both hate spelling but relish athletics and sketching. Mitch has a handle on the alphabet and is getting help in class with phonics. He gave Becky some hints and tricks that made the little black scribbles hold still. By the end of second grade the letters began behaving for Becky, and Mitch was her best old friend.

Vacation

Ben and Josh share a passion for travel. They passed their college admission tests and went on vacation. Both have construction jobs with the Sanitation Commission in June. With some cash from that job and the rest of vacation off, they are set to travel. Their parents have no objections, so with a recitation of restrictions, they gave their permission.

Transportation is no problem. Both Ben and Josh ride bicycles, and they are in top physical condition. Prime consideration will be given to the evasion of traffic congestion. They can make the ride in ten sections of about fifty miles, depending on their conditioning and the elements. Ben and Josh packed a pup tent with the intention of camping, and with a small collection of clothes and provisions, they set off on their expedition.

Cycling against the wind was an aggravation, but the trip met their expectations. With close attention to accident prevention, their vacation was a success with no complications.

The Invention

Cindy drove to a physics convention in Tampa to put on a demonstration of her invention. It is an odd contraption, a wild collection of tubes and wires. When she added drops of pink solution into its holding tank and gave it an injection of a phosphate solution, the eruption was extremely impressive!

An examination by judges from the entire nation resulted only in expressions of confusion. They asked Cindy about the pink solution and the composition of the tanks and needles. Her graphic explanation left blank stares on their faces. The judges' decision was to give her a trophy and a citation, *"In recognition of her contribution to physics."* The judges' imaginations were evident in the best tradition of the national convention.

While on her trip home, Cindy stopped for a picnic in celebration of the citation. In the middle of the park she gave herself a long pat on the back.

The Farm

To study the art of farming, Bill spent some time last March on the farm with his Uncle Charles and Charles' wife Martha. Carla is one of their farm hands. Sparky is their dog. He barks a lot.

On the farm they all get up when it is still dark and the stars are still in the sky. Uncle Charles sets the alarm and says, "It's smart to get a quick start." Farming is a hard and harsh life, most of all at harvest time. The farm hands spend part of the time in the barn or barnyard. They'll use a large garden cart to move stuff from the yard to the barn. Much of the time is spent cutting brush or fixing fences and gates.

Charles and Martha have four sons: Bob, Bart, Ken, and Mark. The sons help on the farm only at harvest time. Mark drives an old sedan and the car starts hard most of the time. Bart has a large scar on his arm where a big bar fell on him in the barn. He must have a charmed life because it didn't harm him badly. Bob and Ken are smart. They don't do much farming; they mostly rest.

The best part of farm life is going to the market in Fargo with Carla. After the garden produce is sold, everyone picnics in the park.

Cornell

Cornell is a fine place for both study and sports. Zelda went there to study. Norma went for sports.

Zelda is from York; Norma was born in Cork, Ireland, but lives with her family in Portland. They met on the Cornell campus and planned to live in the same north wing of the dorm. The two of them got an old car with a ragtop that was badly worn and torn. Plus it had a horn like a sick cornet. They could ill afford it, but that corny horn was what sold them on it. They had to inform Cornell that they had the car on campus.

Norma had to report for sports and was so tired that she had a bad time getting up in the morning for class. She spent a lot of time at the sorority and even made trips in the car to the Stork Club in the city. Zelda would study with her and give her what support she could. Even so, Norma came up short. Her grades were so bad that she had to quit. When she left Cornell, Zelda was forlorn, but Norma gave her the old car and said she would reform and come back to Cornell in the fall.

Sally the Clerk

Sally has a job as salesclerk in the plant section of a big home center. Herb, the boss, tells his clerks that they must be well versed in all plants. This includes a wide range, from roses and mums to ferns and potted herbs. In the spring the department acts as host to the Civic Club. The club members come in like a herd of cattle, and Sally has to serve soft drinks and cakes to them all. This gets on her nerves, and she is apt to get a bit terse with them, even quite stern if they grab more cakes than they should. Sally suspects that the members bring in plant germs from their homes.

Sally is on good terms with most of the clerks, but she thinks Herb, her boss, is a jerk. He smiles like a nerd as he sits on his tall perch at the exit to take in the cash. Often Sally is on the verge of quitting, but she loves plants and is close friends with the other clerks that are there. Most of all, however, there are not many other jobs to be had.

First Circus

On her third birthday, Bert went with his little girl, Irma, to her first circus. They sat in the first level, but Irma kept flirting with a kid named Kirk. Bert had to get firm with Kirk and Irma. Kirk was quite persistent.

When she got thirsty, they went to the concession stand. Bert got her a hamburger and a huge cup of soda. Bert and Irma did not return to the first level where Kirk was, but found a spot on the third level. Irma squirmed so much that the drink spilled on her skirt and on Bert's shirt. Bert kept a lid on his temper.

Irma liked to watch the big black panther in its cage. She tossed bits of her burger to the edge of the cage. This just made the large cat surly and hungry.

What she liked most at the circus were the thirty white birds that chirped as they whirled in a big circle over the Big Top.

On the trip home Irma didn't stir. She was hot and dirty from the circus and slept on the whole trip home. That's just fine with Bert.

Clinic Burglars

Beth is a nurse. She stops at the clinic on Thursday to visit and chat with the sick. On this Thursday she saw two sturdy men lurking at the curve in the path to the clinic. One had on a purple vest and a fur cap. The other had no hat but had long curls. She asked if she could help them, but all they did was murmur something like a curse. Beth kept a strong grip on her purse and went on. She told Dr. Murphy of the two burly men, but she did not want to burden him further and could not furnish a description of their faces.

The next Thursday, Beth had made her parsnip and turnip salad to take to the sick and had forgotten the two furtive men. At the clinic, Dr. Murphy told her that two men had burst into the clinic and stolen some small items. They did not take much, but they did hurl mud at the murals. The men were more vandals than burglars.

Morris

Chuck and Terry Herron live in a state wildlife territory. All animals are their pets. They have a barrel full of bran and millet on their terrace to help carry the birds over the cold winters. A sluggish terrapin they call Hurry lives in the pond. Inside they have two pets: a Kerry Terrier named Mr. Barret and a kitten named Sherry. They all lived in merry harmony until they got Morris.

Morris is a parrot with a stock of profane phrases, an arrogant disposition and a terrible temper. He loves to strut in front of the mirror, and he will attack anything furry. He once terrorized a visitor by diving at her fur collar. Another time he attacked a skunk with sorry results. Mr. Barret lives in terror of Morris, and Sherry will scurry under the sofa to escape him. Morris is fed chopped herring and a porridge of rice and fresh carrots, but he prefers bran and berry jam. The Herrons worry that Morris will embarrass them with his torrent of salty curses when the minister visits. They have been tutoring him to correct this, but even the Wilson program has not helped ... not yet.

Doctor Windsor

Doctor Adam Windsor was the only doctor in the tiny village of Plum Harbor. He was an old bachelor, sang tenor with more vigor than ability, and rode a motorbike with red reflectors. He was a regular spectator at the village sports contests and a frequent visitor to the barber shop of the village where he told tales of the past with fervor and humor.

As the only medical doctor in Plum Harbor, people would go to Dr. Windsor for all their illnesses, from minor cuts to the flu. If it was a major problem, he would send folks to the hospital in Ann Arbor. To Dr. Windsor the beggar and the senator were the same, and he held no favor for one over the other. No labor was withheld from the villagers. Sometimes Dr. Windsor made his medical calls on his motorbike, wearing goggles and a visor. Those motorbike visits were popular with older villagers who didn't have the vigor to get to the doctor alone. They called him 'The Protector.' He was not just the pride of the village, and a pillar of the community, he was a stellar doctor too.

May Day

Ray was late getting home. He had to stay late at his shop in Back Bay to pay bills. He lay back on the day bed for a rest and dozed off. Then, on the way home, he ran into a traffic jam at Fenway with a Red Sox game. He called Kay from a pay phone to tell her of his delay and to say he would be late. Kay was not at home and there was no way to relay the message to her. Her cat had strayed off and got sprayed by a skunk, and she had taken it to the vet.

Ray had planned to take Kay for a May Day dinner at the Wayside Inn. By the time they both got home, it was late and their nerves were frayed. They decided to stay home and hit the hay. They can go to the Wayside Inn on a better day.

Mail Train

There is just one daily train to the little village of Brain Cove, Maine. It is a branch off the main line and is called the mail train. Besides the mail, it brings in sacks of grain, paints and stains, lumber and nails, buckets and pails, sailcloth, and even bait for the lobster pots.

The train's rails are laid over a soggy wetland plain. A big rain can detain the train as it crosses that section or can even derail it! This explains why the citizens of Brain Cove never raise strong hopes of getting things on time. They just wait with faith at the station, hoping that the train will make it across the plain. Sometimes they wait in vain, and they always complain.

It is not fair that the train gets such faint praise from the people of Brain Cove. The train moves at a snail's pace, but it rarely fails to complete its trip. The trainmen are not well paid and should be praised for remaining on the job. The people of Brain Cove should stop complaining and be thankful that they have any train service at all.

Smoked Turkey

The Bradley family had a big turkey dinner for Thanksgiving. They invited the Whitneys and the Hersheys from up the valley. Shirley was stuck in the galley making the dinner. She stuffed the turkey with wild rice, barley, chestnuts, sage and parsley. While she stuffed and baked the turkey, the rest of them played volleyball in the side yard. Charley and his two kids, Barney and Harley, were matched up against the Whitney twins and the Hershey girls.

When dinner was on the table, Charley started a nice fire in the fireplace. In a short time the ranch was so smoky, everyone had to escape to the open air. An osprey had made its nest on the chimney top and blocked the draft. They ate their turkey dinner under the volleyball net in the side yard. Charley pitched the osprey nest off the chimney and opened the draft. He said, "Next Thanksgiving, we'll not have smoked turkey!"

Kathleen and Lee

Kathleen was the golf star at Greenville Prep. In the match between Greenville and Aberdeen, she had to make a short speech as the golfers started off on the first tee. Lee happened to see Kathleen there, and she swept him off his feet. To him, she is a queen. Lee gave her a score of fifteen on a scale of one to ten. He waited to see her tee off, then he ran after the match to see her again on the green. Lee began to sneeze and wheeze from all the grass pollen, so he left.

Lee had a chance to meet Kathleen after the match. She was with three girls who seemed to give cold stares. That left him in the deep freeze. He was speechless and began to feel like a hayseed.

Lee spotted Kathleen's name on the list of Greenville golfers. Her name had the number seventeen after it. Lee is sixteen and a track star at Aberdeen. He's not afraid to date a girl who's seventeen. Lee charmed one of the girls and got Kathleen's phone number at home.

The track meet between Greenville and Aberdeen is next week. Lee would call and see if Kathleen could go to that track meet. Lee began to feel the deep freeze melt away.

Mr. Fleet Feet

The track meet between Aberdeen and Greenville is on Tuesday, ten days after the golf match at Greenville. Kathleen said she would keep her date with Lee and cheer for him. It's true that he's fast and was due to win, so he wanted Kathleen to see why they call him "Mr. Fleet Feet."

Along the avenue, on his way to the track meet, Lee felt a tug on his coattail. It was Kathleen. He spun to greet her, but she gave his hand a squeeze, turned toe and ran off. She was indeed true to her agreement. To Lee, Kathleen was like a fresh breeze.

Lee won three blue ribbons in his three events. Aberdeen succeeded in winning the meet with Greenville. Lee peered up into the stands seeking Kathleen. There she was, sitting between the girls with cold stares. Lee hoped to rescue Kathleen from them, so he met the three of them under the big oak tree on the campus green. Kathleen told Lee she was sixteen. The seventeen on the Greenville club's sheet was her golf handicap! That made Lee feel a little sheepish, but her sweet smile made him feel better.

Kathleen still seemed like a queen to Lee.

The Donahue Ranch

Roscoe and Joan Donahue live on a ranch in Whiskey Valley with their teenage children, Moe and Wesley. On the ranch they have a donkey, two horses, three dogs, and a cat. The place teems with white-tailed deer (buck and doe). The land is quite dry most of the time, but the deep valley to their west turns into a raging river due to the spring rains.

They have a big kidney-shaped pond in their backyard which they use both for swimming and for irrigation of their garden. The pond is fenced and locked, and Roscoe and Joan keep the key. They have strict safety rules for swimming: There will be no running or monkey business, and no person may swim alone.

The Donahues strung up a trolley with a pulley to let the kids slide into the pond. The kids cling to the trolley and glide along its wire and then drop with a splash into the middle of the pond.

One day in the garden, Moe stubbed his toe on the hoe. He made an undue moan and groan over it, and his toe got all black and blue. Despite all his woeful complaining, he continued to take his turns on the trolley.

From time to time, Moe and Wesley ask the Sloan kids over for a barbecue in the side yard of the ranch. Everyone plays hockey and volleyball in the alley behind the corral.

The Floating Toad

Joe's boat is called the Floating Toad. She's a big, blue boat used for shipping coal. She is made of oak and is due for a coat of paint. Joe Sloan is her skipper; his wife Sue is first mate.

On their last trip, Joe and Sue floated along the Atlantic coast. At Oak Bluffs, they picked up a huge cargo of loam and oats. It was there that Joe slipped on a bar of soap and broke his toe. A friend came to their rescue and loaned them his van so that Joe and Sue could roam the avenues of Oak Bluffs. As they roamed, they picked up barbecued beef sandwiches and had a picnic along the roadside. They continued their trip from Oak Bluffs with the boat bobbing like a bloated toad due to its large load. Joe was able to keep it afloat, but they were two days overdue at their final port.

Joe and Sue sold their cargo, and, with the revenue from the sale, they were able to pay off the loan on their boat.

A Letter to Joyce

Joe was at his desk poised to scratch off a long overdue letter to Joyce, but now there was so much noise he could not even think. His pals, full of joy and in fine voice, had just come back from a wedding party, and it was useless to argue or try to subdue them.

Joyce, his girl, was living in Detroit. She had sprained her ankle joint and broken her toe in an accident, and Joe wanted to help her. He had sent her some ointment and pain pills and planned to join her before long in Detroit. He also wanted to share a sirloin dinner with her and rejoice over her appointment as president of the oil company. Joyce's study and toil had paid off, and Joe hoped she would continue to pursue her goals. Joe was happy for her and felt that she was an excellent choice for the job. He also wanted to help Joyce with her garden. With a bum joint and a broken toe, she could not very well handle a hoe and spade. Once planted, the soil would just need to be kept moist.

Later, when the members of the wedding retinue were more subdued, Joe finished his letter, ending it with, "Your true love, Joe."

Poise

One spring day in the backyard, while giving little Molly a lesson in poise, Sue fell in the moist grass and landed in a mud puddle. She soiled her skirt and got a nasty twist in her hip joint. It was a woeful example of poise and spoiled her lesson.

Later that day her dog Roscoe, a pointer, got into some rat poison and had to be taken to the vet. On the way Sue's car began to boil over. She ran to a pay phone to call for help, but she had no coins. At last, a truck came to her rescue and got her to the Blue Hill Avenue Shop. The shop put the car up on a hoist and installed an ignition, a fan belt, and a coil. The car was also due for an oil change. It cost a lot, but Sue could not argue. She had no choice. She then continued to the vet.

Despite feeling a bit unglued, Sue made an appointment to join her friends for a barbecue dinner. They met at a small, subdued place where they did not have to raise their voices over the noise. In spite of all this turmoil, Sue could rejoice in the fact that little Molly had all the poise she needed to avoid mud puddles and Roscoe had survived the rat poison.

Floyd and Oyster

Bob and Joyce Truesdale live in Boylston. They have a boy named Floyd, who is the joy of their life. They also have a dog named Oyster. They got the dog from an oyster fisherman on Cape Cod, which is why they call him Oyster.

Bob is employed by the True Blue Toy Company where he has been a loyal employee for a long time. His job is to see that the toys are safe. He must make sure the paint and glue have no toxic or harmful residue. Bob also enjoys music and plays the oboe. He and Joe Doyle conduct the song and dance revue at the barbecue the company puts on every spring. The revenue goes to the Homeless Rescue Fund.

Bob brings toys home from the shop. Floyd and Oyster enjoy the toys. They play hard with them and at times get so wild with their play that they destroy them. That annoys Joyce, but Bob says if Floyd and Oyster cannot destroy them, they can be sure the toys are strong. Floyd is happy to have the toys, and the shop is happy to have the toys tested. The employees in the shop call it the "Truesdale Test."

The Gaults

The Gault family lived in Austria. Paul Gault had an auto body shop and was also the author of a small weekly paper. His wife, Maude, and her aunt ran a small automatic laundry to augment their income. Their daughter Paula ran a public sauna behind the laundry and also kept an audit of all their records. Their joint revenue was small, but they were happy in their Austrian home.

When the enemy launched their attack on Austria, it was the beginning of woe for the Gaults. The army men hauled Paul from his auto shop, told him he was in default of tax payments which were long overdue, and accused him of being a spy. None of this was true. Paul did not have a clue of what the problem was. He offered to discontinue the weekly paper if the army men felt it was at fault, but it was useless to argue with such a grim foe. The men brutally assaulted Paul. He defended himself in toe to toe battle with them, but they did at last subdue him. Maude shut off the laundry faucets and rushed to Paul. All of the Gaults were upset at such a brutal mauling. They could not understand the cause of the assault, but it taught them that they could no longer pursue their life in Austria.

The Gault's Escape

For a month the Gaults planned their escape. They had to use caution because the authorities haunted them constantly. Little by little, they saved their money and put it in the vault at the bank. They got fraudulent passports from a man who called himself only "Rescue." The passports had almost faultless autographs of the top authority.

At last, under a blue August sky, the Gaults packed what they could carry and marched undaunted to the border. There was a long pause while one austere sentry muttered something inaudible and seemed to argue with another sentry. At last the sentry decided that the passports were authentic, and they let the Gaults pass.

The Gaults had to abandon their auto shop, the laundry and Paula's sauna. It had been a long haul, and even after their little family passed the sentry point, they didn't feel safe. They kept glancing back thinking someone was there to pursue them.

The Dirty Hawk

In the old West, Bill Hawkins ran a pawn shop called The Dirty Hawk. It was an awful joint. On the wall he had scrawled: "We argue but we do not brawl."

But brawls did happen. One day Bill was off at the sawmill and left his wife, Dawn, minding the store. She was at her desk setting values on the pawned items they had accrued. Hacksaw Jones was playing a friendly game of five card draw at a table with his pals. When Joe McGraw came in, they had to discontinue the game. All but Jones ran for the exits, and Dawn crawled under her desk. McGraw and Jones were mortal foes. There was sure to be a brawl. McGraw was big and brawny, a man of little virtue, hated by all. Jones was scrawny but quick. The two of them kicked and clawed and pawed at one another until the law came to subdue them. The lawmen called it a draw. McGraw went his way, the game started up again, and Dawn crawled from under her desk to continue tagging the merchandise.

This all happened long ago, and this story may not be true. The Dirty Hawk is now called The White Hawk and is located on a wide and fashionable avenue in a modern, big city. It is freshly painted and sells coffee, dainty cakes and sweet muffins.

The Blounts

The Blounts live about a mile south of the county line. Jane Blount is tiny, not much over a hundred pounds. She spends her time in the kitchen, sweeping and dusting. Joe Blount is big and stout with a pot belly that hangs over his belt. He is handy around the house and is able to fix just about anything. They are proud of their house.

Joe has a job at the foundry; Jane works part-time at the flour mill. Joe can be a grouch at times and shouts at the kids if they do not mind. Their two boys, Little Joe and Roscoe, are seven and nine. They have to shovel snow, mow the lawn, and haul the trash. They argue about the chores, but they do them. They have a hound they call Pounce because of the way he pounces on mice. He is of value as a mouse trap and may account for the fact that there are no mice in their house.

On any fine, cloudless Saturday, Joe may glance up at the blue sky and announce in a loud voice that they are overdue for a fishing trip. The boys may argue about chores, but not about fishing. Within an hour they are off. Jane prefers to stay home for a restful day by herself.

Brown's Flowers

Sue Brown has a farm. She raises flowers to sell in the town markets. For her family she keeps a cow, a hen called Perdue, some baby chicks, and an old sow named Wilbur. The Browns also have a hound dog named Bowser. Sue's children have a pet owl named Moe and a raven named Poe. Moe and Poe are kept in the barn. Sue's farm is on the edge of town. The town frowns on farm animals and will not allow them within the town limits. Sue will not argue with this ruling. She says she would rather not live in town anyhow.

Sue has a windmill to pump from her well. She depends on the spring rains and the windmill to irrigate her gardens, and she uses a hoe and a trowel to keep the weeds down. This way she can continue to keep costs down.

On holidays Sue puts on a gown of a rosy hue and, with a crown of flowers in her hair, goes into town as a clown. She sells bunches of flowers to the happy crowds. The children howl with joy when they see their clown. These trips are of value to Sue from the standpoint of revenue and for public relations as well.

The Big Crow

Anna Harris lives in a house on the banks of the Big Crow River. To her it is just the Crow. It is lined by birch and willow trees and is wide and shallow as it flows slowly below her window. On sunny days it takes on a golden yellow glow. Farther along, the Crow gets so narrow that you can throw a stone across it. There it flows much faster.

Anna had the luck to grow up on the Crow and likes to think of it is her own river. As a child, she would take her rowboat out to catch minnows. She would throw grass seed out, and when the minnows came up, she would catch them in an old pillow case.

As a child, Anna got pocket money by mowing lawns. Her mom said a girl should not mow lawns. Anna did not think that was true and would argue with her mom about it. When Anna had to give up mowing, she sold minnows for live bait to fishermen. For a little extra cash, she would show them the best place to fish below the dam.

Anna has grown old now. She sits at her open window as the setting sun glows on the river. As darkness falls, she gazes at the stars that reflect on the river and remembers her many happy days as a child on her own Big Crow.

Granny Loo

Lola Loomis still lives with her children in Toledo. When her grandchildren were little they could not pronounce her name, so they just called her Granny Loo. Lola used to play the bassoon with the Cleveland Symphony, and she still plays it from time to time. She also is talented at making woven fabrics on her loom. She makes scarves, blankets and wall hangings for her family and friends.

Lola has a little room of her own where she keeps her bassoon and her loom. The room has such a low roof that most people have to stoop to get in, but Lola is shorter than most and fits just fine.

Lola is happy and helpful much of the time, but when the moon is full or when her foot swells up with the gout, she gets moody and grouchy. Then she goes to her room and plays her bassoon or gets out her spools of woolens and sits at her loom. She says it lifts her out of the blues.

Lola's grandchildren love her even when she is grouchy, but when she gets moody and shuts herself up in her room, they say she is having her Loony Time. That is when they call her Loony Loo.

Aunt Loo's School

Long ago Aunt Loo ran a school up in Seattle. It was just a single room with a tool shed and was located on the shore of Puget Sound. There was a bell on the roof and a box for the kids' boots on the front stoop. A big potbelly stove kept the room toasty on the cold winter days. The kids hung their coats and jackets over the stove to dry. Children of all ages sat in the one room, and Aunt Loo gave out lessons that fit their different levels. At noon the children sat around the potbelly stove and ate the sandwiches they had packed from home.

Aunt Loo loved animals. She kept a raccoon, a tame goose, and a pet rooster and had a stuffed hoot owl in a bamboo cage. She had to shoo the rooster out of the room by noon before her afternoon class could start. She kept corn to feed the raccoon and the rooster. The tame goose ran loose and lived on grass and roots that it dug up from the bottom of the sound.

The children got a solid foundation in their ABC's with Aunt Loo, but of special value were her lessons in the love and care of animals.

Aunt Loo's Zoo

One day the kids led a baby moose to school with a noose around its neck. It had stepped into a trap and had cut a big split in its hoof. The kids called it their "moose papoose." They groomed that poor little moose with the school room broom and fed it with a spoon. They kept it in the tool shed with the rooster. Its hoof soon got well, and Aunt Loo told them that they could not continue to keep the moose in the shed; they had to turn it loose. She said it was foolish and unsafe to keep a wild moose penned up. It is true that a blow from the moose's hoof could spell doom to any kid that got in the way.

There was such a hue and cry at letting the moose go free that Aunt Loo had to get the children a dog. The dog was named Moose and was kept in the tool shed with the rooster. Aunt Loo's school was fast becoming Aunt Loo's Zoo!

Becky's Cook Book

Becky is not a crook, but it did look as if she had taken the book. The store owner had been over every foot of the bookstore looking for it. At last he found Becky sitting in a dark nook at the foot of the wooden steps with the book. At first the store owner had mistaken Becky for a pile of coats. He nudged Becky with his toe and asked her if she had paid for the book. She just shook her head and hid under her hood. Becky said she wanted to find out how to cook so she could help her mom, and looking at a cook book seemed like a good way to get information. Becky did not argue with the owner. She stood up and put the book back in the rack. She had played hooky from Miss Brook's class because she wanted to find out how to cook, but she had not intended to take the book. Becky is a good girl, and in due time she will be a good cook.

Cruising with Eugene

Eugene was just out of engineering school. His first job was with a crew digging a sluiceway to flush out polluted low lands. Eugene was a raw recruit, and he soon found that the job did not suit him. It was a dirty job, he had a feud with the crew boss and the bugs were a constant nuisance. Eugene began to feel like a sewer rat. As soon as he could accrue some cash, he drew out his savings, quit his job, and went in pursuit of something more suitable. It turned out to be a shrewd maneuver.

At the employment agency Eugene ran into Sue, a girl he had dated at Purdue. Sue had just landed a spot as a waitress on a new cruise ship that sailed back and forth to Europe. The ship needed a few deck stewards, and Eugene decided that would be a good job for him: he liked to travel and he could be around Sue. Eugene had always hoped to go to Europe someday, and this trip would be at a price he could afford. He grabbed the job.

Taking the job as a steward was another shrewd move. On the cruises, Eugene's friendship with Sue grew. At first she felt neutral about Eugene, but by the third trip she consented to marry him. Eugene and Sue plan to continue on the cruise ship until they can afford to get a boat of their own.

A Bleak Year for the Beals

The Beals have not had an easy year. Joe Beal had a pile of overdue bills that he was unable to pay. Molly, his wife, lost her teaching job. Their pet beagle had fleas, and they had to keep her on a leash.

Until disaster struck, Robert, their son, had been the leading hitter on the Eagles, his little league team. Last year the Eagles had a winning streak, beating each of the other teams. They had dreams of doing as well this season. Then, just before April, Robert got a deep cut and bruise on his right thigh and was lame for most of the season. He could only limp around on the side lines and was of little value to the team. This was a blow to him and to the team as well.

Then Robert's little sister Jean got sick with the measles. Measles is a grave disease. Jean got so frail she could hardly speak. At the peak of her disease all she could eat was thin cream of wheat, fruit juice and weak tea. Joe and Molly feared for her life. They had to keep her room dark with the window shades down, and tiptoe around so as not to disturb her sleep. Jean did survive, but she wound up with a neuritis that left her with a slight hearing defect. Things were indeed bleak for the Beals that year.

The Beals at the Beach

The Beals lived within easy reach of the seashore. When little Jean was over the measles, Bob decided they were due for a vacation. They could by no means afford a cruise to Europe. The beach was always a real treat for them, but even a week at the beach seemed out of reach. Bob's neighbor felt sorry for the Beals with all their bad luck and came to their rescue by suggesting that they use his new beach house. This seemed like an ideal plan, and it pleased the family. They quickly packed their swimming suits, beach togs, sun tan lotion, dark glasses, good books, and blue jeans and, at the last minute, they threw in some beach towels. Bob took some vacation time from his job, and the Beals piled into their large van and were off to the beach.

At the beach, Robert had to continue his exercises for his bruised thigh. Jean got stronger, ate well and began to gain back the weight she had lost. She even recovered her hearing. The Beals all swam, basked in the sun and got well rested. They were forever grateful to their kind neighbor who made such a fine vacation possible for them.

Ben and Heather

Ben and Heather have a homestead at the head of Bear Valley about a hundred miles west of Eureka. Their home is on the breast of a hill surrounded by grassy meadows that spread out on all sides. At the bottom of the hill a line of trees marks where Dead Man's Creek cuts into the valley as it threads its way to the big river beyond. In their back yard Ben and Heather have a fruit orchard with apple, pear and plum trees. Pheasant, grouse, and quail are plentiful and feed on the seed Heather throws out to them. Heather has a garden on the south side of the house. Ben keeps a few cows for their own milk supply, and sheep graze in the meadow to keep the grass mowed. Their three children are grown and have left home. One child lives in Eureka and another lives in Eugene, Oregon. Their third child was killed in an accident in Europe many years ago. Their home, already paid for, is their only wealth, and they treasure it. Ben and Heather have their health and find peace in their homestead on the hill.

Ben and Heather (continued)

Ben is a big man, heavy and overweight, and a little deaf. He gets short of breath if he runs around too much. He wears a leather jacket whatever the weather. Ben has a steady job at the Bear Valley Ranch and takes wealthy dudes on trips in the valley.

Heather is a slight woman with a pleasant manner. She bakes her own bread and makes a savory vegetable beef stew. Her cakes are as fluffy as feathers and have picked off blue ribbons at the state and county fairs. She is handy with the needle and thread and keeps their homestead tidy and fresh, always ready for visitors to drop in from the surrounding ranches.

Ben looks like a big brute, but he is soft and gentle with Heather. He is protective of her almost beyond reason. He will worry if he thinks she stands in the way of harm or injury or gets so much as a slight bruise. Heather is really quite strong and healthy and cannot understand why Ben is so attentive. She says he gets to be a nuisance with all his worry, but she does not complain. She seems to enjoy it.

NOTES

NOTES

NOTES